# Before You Leap:

## *Uncommon Things You Should Know Before You Become An Entrepreneur*

Steven Imke

Produced in the United States of America

First Printing, 2016

ISBN-13: 978-1534682702
ISBN-10: 1534682708

KSI Enterprises
395 Scrub Oak Circle
Monument CO 80132

www.SteveBizBlog.com

# About the Author

Steve's first foray into the world of small business came when he was an Invisible Fencing dealer. He operated this business on a part-time basis while remaining employed by a Fortune 500 company called Digital Equipment Corporation (DEC). While the Invisible Fencing business was not very successful for Steve, it was a valuable opportunity for him to learn important lessons about business in a relatively low-risk environment.

After ending his relationship with Invisible Fencing, he worked on a business plan for a new business idea and waited for the right opportunity to present itself. In 1994, DEC fell on hard times. Instead of bemoaning this turbulent economic tide, Steve capitalized on this opportunity. He quit his day job at DEC to found Horizon Interactive, a documentation and training company. In fact, Horizon Interactive became a vendor for DEC.

Over the next few years, Steve and his partners executed the business plan. The business grew to over $3 million in annual sales and opened offices in several states. Horizon Interactive's success drew the attention of Interleaf, a publicly held company out of Massachusetts. In 1999, Interleaf acquired Horizon Interactive.

As part of the acquisition, Steve was offered the position of VP of Operations for their services division. Under his leadership, Interleaf acquired two more businesses like

Horizon Interactive. The company grew the services side of the business from a combined $8 million in revenue to over $32 million in sales during the next two years.

In 2001, Interleaf was acquired by Broadvision, a California company during the height of the dot com era. Broadvision primarily acquired Interleaf for their XML engineers who worked on the product side of the business. Needing to divest himself from the services business, Steve and a former business partner acquired the assets of Interleaf's service business and started IC Interactive. They operated the business for a few more years until they sold it in 2003.

Being a serial entrepreneur, Steve has started and still operates three different businesses. One of his businesses is focused on real estate. The second one is focused on oil and gas. His third business is a company designed to help high net-worth investors understand the ins and outs of investing in oil and gas direct participation programs.

Steve has volunteered his time since 2003 as a mentor for SCORE, a local organization dedicated to helping entrepreneurs. He has acted as their Chapter Chairman for several years. He is also an advisory board member of his local Small Business Development Center (SBDC). In additions to his advisory role, he also acts as a counselor for the SBDC since 2003. In 2012, Steve acted as the interim director of SBDC while they conducted a national search for a permanent director. Currently, Steve is the Entrepreneurship Director at Pikes Peak Community College and writes a daily blog about small businesses.

Steve is a flaming dyslexic, which has its good points and bad points. Growing up, he remembers undergoing a board of education evaluation. When asked to draw a tree, Steve drew a series of concentric rings. When asked about his drawing, he said the rings were what you see when you cut down the tree and look at the stump. These rings tell the entire life story of the tree. The evaluator told his parents he was not normal. He should be more like the other kids and draw the tree from the side view.

However, rather than conform to the crowd, Steve embraced his out-of-the-box thinking as an asset. The upside of being dyslexic is exceptional spatial awareness and problems solving skills. Dyslexics develop these heightened skills since they are forced from an early age to compensate for things they do not do well.

Being a dyslexic in school prevented Steve from becoming a good reader. Even today, spelling and grammar are not his strong suits. Academically, Steve struggled in traditional schools. When he graduated from high school, he knew that a traditional classroom education was not for him so he joined the United States Coast Guard to learn a trade. Graduating near the top of his class in tech school, Steve realized that he learned by doing.

Steve tends to be an overly logical person. He likes to explore, document, and measure nearly every aspect of a project to find out what works and what does not. He has a propensity to focus on understanding why things are the way they are rather than how to duplicate what others have already done. Once Steve obtains a reasonable level of mastery in a specific subject area, he internalizes the knowledge and moves on to his next area of interest.

Everything of substance Steve knows about small business initially began by him reading books, listening to audiobooks, or watching others. He internalizes the salient points, then rolls up his sleeves and puts them into practice in his own business. Once Steve perfects a lesson, he makes it a point to document it and then share it with others. He calls these "Sea Stories," leveraging his old Coast Guard days. In addition to sharing his knowledge, this practice serves to further solidify his learning in his own mind while continuing to grow his knowledge base. In this way, Steve has codified over more than a decade's worth of his small business knowledge in the various books he has written.

This process has served Steve pretty well. By the time he was 42 years old, Steve had reached the point where he no longer needed to work for money. Passing this income milestone has not only allowed him the luxury to spend even more time to ponder and digest life's lessons, but also the freedom to tell it like it is without the fear of losing his job. He proudly wears jeans nearly every day. He also sports facial hair to remind himself and others that being a nonconformist and not subscribing to traditional viewpoints has its merits for entrepreneurs.

Steve constantly reads and listens to non-fiction audiobooks about politics or business related topics. He consumes current events from a huge basket of news sources every day so he can relate their messages in new and innovative ways. After internalizing a message and testing new theories, he shares his new-found wisdom with people willing to listen.

Since 2003, Steve has mentored and counseled thousands of fledgling entrepreneurs through his volunteer efforts with SCORE and SBDC. He has volunteered his expertise to help organizations like ARC, a program which helps individuals with developmental disabilities.

As cliché as it may sound, Steve is at the point in his life where it is all about using his skills and knowledge to help others to succeed. Steve never expects anything in return, but simply enjoys the appreciation he receives from the people he has helped and lives vicariously through their success. For Steve, sharing his knowledge is akin to the feeling a billionaire might have handing out $100 bills to random strangers on the street. He knows that by sharing some of the wisdom he has accumulated with clients, he can often make a positive difference in their lives. Steve is not particularly religious so helping entrepreneurs is his way of giving back and making a significant impact on the world around him.

# Table of Contents

Diversify: Good Advice For Stocks, Good Advice For Business....................................................................1
Go Niche or Go Broke.......................................2
Good Cooks Do Not Make Good Restaurateurs............3
Industry Knowledge Is Overrated...................................4
You Should Be Getting Paid Twice............................5
What is Your Entrepreneurial Driver?........................6
Have you Defined your Leap of Faith Assumptions?.....7
Failing Your Way to Wealth..........................................8
Be an Inch Wide And a Mile Deep...............................9
Ever Consider a Co-Packer?........................................10
Exposing Yourself........................................................12
Academic Education Overrated?..................................14
What Do You See In The Mirror?................................15
All In or All Out...........................................................17
Something Never Taught in an MBA Program............19
Learn To Supplement Your Income Before Taking The Plunge.........................................................................20
Who is Your Jester?.....................................................21
Veterans Make Good Entrepreneurs............................22
Business Ownership Changes the Entire Family..........24
A Lesson From The Ship Of Gold...............................25
Salary vs. Standard of Living.......................................28
Being an Inventor Does Not Make You an Entrepreneur ....................................................................................30
Do You Leverage Group Think?..................................32
Take Baby Steps...........................................................33
Buy Four Green Houses Before You Buy a Red Hotel. 34
Do You Have Access To Capital?.................................36
Do You Have What It Takes To Be a Successful?.........37
Are You Committed?....................................................39
How to Leverage a Turning Tide.................................41
What an Ear of Corn Can Teach Us.............................43

Challenges of Creating a New Category......................45
Free SBA Tool to See How your Business Stacks Up  47
Demand Curve Demographics......................................48
What We Can Learn From The Texas Cattle Industry.  50
Ignorance Can Be Bliss................................................53
The Curse of Knowledge.............................................54
Rise of the Micro Business..........................................57
Number One Stated Reason For Not Starting a Business
....................................................................................59
A Great Idea Is Not Enough........................................60
Testing the Market......................................................61
Diversify Your Small Business Risk............................63
How to Choose the Right Occupation..........................64
Tacit vs. Explicit Knowledge......................................66
Belief vs. Assumption.................................................68
A Source of Innovation...............................................70
Primary vs. Secondary Employers...............................71
Don't Be a Gold Digger...............................................74
Four Questions Before You Start Something New........75
The Drug Dealer's Mindset.........................................77
Your Best Chance to Succeed in Small Business..........80
Value of Due Diligence...............................................83
Funding Plan..............................................................84
Retirement Account Funds New Business  .................86
Using a Self-Directed IRA to Fund Your Business.......88
Using a 401k Loan to Fund Your Business...................90
Get Your Private Employer to Pay Your Start-up Costs 92
Cash Flow Quadrant...................................................94
Employee – Cash Flow Quadrant................................96
Self-Employed – Cash Flow Quadrant.........................97
Business Owner – Cash Flow Quadrant.......................99
Investor – Cash Flow Quadrant.................................101
Business Evolution Series..........................................104
Stage 1: The Oracles of Business..............................106
Stage 2: The Generals of Business.............................108
Stage 3: The Athletes and Performers of Business......111

Stage 4: The Guardians of Business............................113

## Diversify: Good Advice For Stocks, Good Advice For Business

Once a month I sit on a military transition panel where the audience includes perhaps a dozen or so folks considering following an entrepreneurial path after separating from the armed forces. I often ask them why are they considering going into business rather than "working for the man," as they say. I get the usual platitudes like "I want be my own boss" or "I want to control my own destiny".

The fact is that these are not good reasons. To help them understand why not, I ask them "How many of you own stock". Everybody's hands go up. I then ask "Are you invested in the stock of only one company". Nobody raises their hand. I ask them "Why", and they say "diversification." I then ask "Is your job income diversified or does it come from only one company", and the light bulbs come on.

For me, one of the best reason for taking on the risk of starting a business is to have diversified income sources. If you have a dozen customers and one chooses not to renew your contact for reasons outside your control, you still have eleven more customers. You may have to cut a few expenses until you find a replacement for the customer you lost, but you will still be able to earn an income.

*Is your income stream diversified?*

## *Go Niche or Go Broke*

Do you think that by claiming that your service business can do everything you will be able to achieve higher revenues? If you feel this way, you are not alone.

Many entrepreneurs feel that by offering more services they will have more income streams, leading to higher overall revenues. However, in practice this is just not true for a small business. Consumers want an expert.

You would never go to a doctor that said "after we finish your physical I can fix your crown". You would figure that if he was a knowledgeable Doctor of Medicine that he could not also be a knowledgeable Dentist. You would simply choose one medical doctor and a different dentist.

To be considered an expert and therefore be worthy of someone buying your services you have to have focus. You must be able to demonstrate that you have the skills that make you better in your specific area of expertise than your competitors.

*Are you spreading yourself out too thin by claiming to be an expert in too many areas?*

## *Good Cooks Do Not Make Good Restaurateurs*

Most businesses are not started by an business people, but by what Michele Gerber, the author of "The E-Myth", calls a "Technician". The technician is a person good at the technical skills the business needs.

A cook is a culinary technician, but the successful restaurateur has no time to cook. They must operate the business and deal with vendors, employees and customers, all while marketing the restaurant and managing its finances.

Most entrepreneurs lack the business knowledge to manage and grow their business, which is a major contributor to the high rate of business failure. The successful entrepreneur needs to value operational skills such as financial, marketing, and sales as much as they value the technical portion of their business if they hope to have any business success.

*Do you have the acumen to start a new venture?*

## Industry Knowledge Is Overrated

When it comes to owning and operating a business, industry knowledge is often not required. In fact, in the case of many franchise-type opportunities, being an expert is considered grounds for non-acceptance.

Jeff Bezos, the founder of Amazon.com, never sold a book. Henry Ford was a farmer.

When it comes to starting a business, industry knowledge is often overrated, while business knowledge is underrated. Before pursuing your entrepreneurial goals, make sure you have adequate business knowledge.

*Are relying solely on your industry knowledge to carry your venture to success?*

## You Should Be Getting Paid Twice

Adam Smith wrote in his book the Wealth of Nations,

> *"The value which the workmen add to the materials, therefore, resolves itself in this case into two parts, of which the one pays their wages, the other the profits of the employer upon the whole stock of materials and wages which he advanced."*

As an entrepreneur, you didn't undertake all the risk of starting a business just to create a job for yourself. As Adam Smith points out, whatever revenue is produced should not only cover the the labor, material, and indirect overhead, but should also provide a return to the owner based on the risk of the investment of his time and treasure to start the business in the first place.

*Are your products and services priced in such a way as to not only pay your wages for working in the business, but providing you an adequate return for the risk capital you had to invest to start and grow your business?*

## What is Your Entrepreneurial Driver?

Most people have a rather vague answer when asked why they are willing to risk so much to be a small business owner. Having interacted with over a thousand entrepreneurs I have found there are four primary drivers that cause a person to follow an entrepreneurial dream. These are:

- Personal fame & recognition,
- Achieving financial independence
- Driving social change
- Attaining job independence.

Not understanding your primary entrepreneurial driver can lead to dissatisfaction and ultimately business failure.

*What is your entrepreneurial driver?*

## *Have you Defined your Leap of Faith Assumptions?*

Many start-up business make huge leap of faith assumptions. By definition a leap of faith is believing in or accepting something without any proof or evidence. These assumptions often feed false conclusions that lead to more assumptions in a vicious cycle.

Consider the leap of faith assumption that the world was flat. It precipitated further assumptions that if you sailed over the horizon you would fall off the world. These false assumptions prevented wise men of the day from considering the seas as possible trade routes to new, yet undiscovered, lands to the West.

When it comes to business, leap of faith assumptions need to be identified and documented in your business plan and methodically tested to prove their validity. If a leap of faith assumption proves to be false the business will need to pivot or risk spending money and effort on an outcome it cannot realistically achieve.

*Do you have a plan to test your leap of faith assumptions?*

## *Failing Your Way to Wealth*

My first small business experience was with an Invisible Fencing franchise. My wife and I operated the business while I continued to maintained a full-time job. At the time I considered myself under-employed. After about five years I lost my franchise due to under-performance since I was unwilling to quite my day job.

Several years later I had an opportunity to start a documentation and training development company. My wife was quick to remind me that the last business I tried was not very successful, to which I replied "but I learned so much from the failed experience that I think I can do much better".

This second company required that I go all-in and quit my corporate job. There were lots of reasons why the second company was much more successful then my first. However, my experience underscores the concept of failing small.

Would-be entrepreneurs are encouraged to start a small business that does not have large upfront costs as a way to learn to understand financials, operational controls, marketing and sales before jumping in with both feet.

*Are there opportunities for you to spread out and try your entrepreneurial wings before leaping from the nest?*

## Be an Inch Wide And a Mile Deep

Many entrepreneurs falsely believe that if they claim that they can do everything they will have more sources of revenue.

The problem is that such statements destroy market credibility and thin out your message so that your message never rises above the din of other companies. You would never hire your landscaper as your financial adviser. You would not think anyone could be an expert in medicine and a good financial adviser as well.

When we hire someone we want to hire a expert, not someone that just dabbles in an area. Furthermore, a key part of marketing is branding. It takes a lots of effort to create brand awareness. You only have so much time and so many resources. If you spread your branding efforts across several expertise areas you will never achieve enough penetration in any one area to be recognized above others offering the same products or services. You will be like the tiny sea mountain that is below the surface of the ocean, never to be seen.

*How can you change your business model to be an inch wide and mile deep?*

### *Ever Consider a Co-Packer?*

So your family says that you make the best food product or beverage and is encouraging you to sell it, but you just don't have the capital to build a commercial facility and hire workers. Why not consider a co-packer or co-bottler?

A co-packer or co-bottler is a company that manufactures and packages food or beverages for its clients. You provide the recipe and packaging specifications, and they produce the finished product for you in whatever quantities you desire. All you have to do is sell the product.

I first learned about contract manufacturing, AKA co-packers/co-bottlers, a few years ago when I was vacationing in the Adirondack mountains. Looking for something to do indoors on a particularly rainy day, we decided to do a factory tour of the West End Brewery in Utica, NY. The brewery was opened in 1853 and is the second oldest family owned brewery in the US. They are known for their Saranac line of beer. As I was watching one of the lines spit out bottles of beer I noticed they were producing a beer with the label Brooklyn Brewery. I was pretty confused and asked our tour guide about it. I learned that West End Brewery is what is known as a co-bottler, and produces craft beer for clients on contract.

By contracting with a co-packer for food or a co-bottler for beverages you can leverage their resources and keep your start up capital requirements low. If the product takes off, then you can invest in your own manufacturing facility to achieve greater margins.

*Could you use the services of a co-packer or co-bottler to test the market for a consumable product idea?*

## Exposing Yourself

The Civil Rights Act of 1964 was an attempt to provide equal rights for black Americans. It expressly prohibited discrimination in voting, education, and public facilities. Although fraught with lots of implementation issues, integration in schools changed many people's mindset about other races.

It is human nature to like "like-minded people". We often erect artificial barriers to segregate "non-like minded people" to keep them out of our network circles. When you understand that our views of the world and how we see opportunities are colored by the company we keep, you can see that by not venturing outside your village of friends leads to group think, and prevents exposure to new ideas.

In the book Who Owns the Ice House, by Clifton Taulbert and Garry Schoeniger, Uncle Cleve, a black man living in the Mississippi delta in the 1950's, refused to be subjected to group think. Rather than work in the cotton fields like everyone else, he chose to break out and became an entrepreneur: an ice distributor.

Since entrepreneurs know that ideas and knowledge are the real drivers of success, they know that group think is their mortal enemy. Rather then be insulated from new ideas, entrepreneurs look for every opportunity to connect with people outside their clique.

*What are you doing to reach out and expose yourself to new people and ideas?*

## Academic Education Overrated?

Many successful entrepreneurs know that being successful is not about academic education. Instead they know that being successful is about focus and persistence.

Many successful entrepreneurs are high school and college dropouts. They quit school because they didn't see the purpose of what they were learning. Many school curriculums are too narrow or too broad in scope. They are also outdated and lack the proper data to teach what it takes to be successful.

Most teachers and professors went to college and upon graduation spent the next 40 years teaching what they learned. They have no idea what it takes to be a successful entrepreneur. While many successful entrepreneurs have a formal education, few credit their success to what they learned in school. Being a successful entrepreneur is less about academic education and more about being focused. You need to do what it takes to achieve your goals.

*Are you banking on academic achievement to make you a successful entrepreneur or are you ready to roll up your sleeves and just do it?*

## *What Do You See In The Mirror?*

America was built on a culture of hard work. American workers work harder then the Germans, the French, and even the Japanese. Even during their leisure time many Americans build furniture and grow gardens just for fun. They coach soccer or baseball teams and volunteer to help non-profit organizations. Overall, most Americans are just not happy sitting still.

The spirit of the entrepreneur permeates America's culture. As entrepreneurs we have a double dose of the hard work ethic that fuels our nation's economic engine.

Many entrepreneurs work fifty to eighty or even more hours per week. When they are not working they are reading books or attend training programs to keep their skills up. I have never met a successful entrepreneur that is truly happy not working on something all the time, even after they retire.

The entrepreneurial spirit is the cornerstone of our nation's economic success. We need to encourage it at every level, including with our kids, to maintain our place as the leader in the world's economy.

*When you look at yourself in the mirror, what do you see?*

*Do you see a warrior with battle scars from his life in the business arena, contributing to our nation's greatness, or do you see a person that has neither seen victory nor defeat, enjoying the fruits of others while secretly coveting what others have obtained?*

## All In or All Out

When Cortés came to the Americas, he feared his army might take the safe option when faced with fierce Aztec warriors and return to Spain rather than continue to fight. Accordingly, he decided to scuttle most of his fleet, thereby removing the safe option for his soldiers. Effectively stranded, his army had no other choice but to succeed in their goal. They had to plunder Aztec gold or die trying. The result was that his expedition succeeded.

In debt financing, lenders generally require a substantial investment from the business owner before they consider extending any type of loan. This practice insures that the debt is secured by the owner's own skin in the game, which dramatically improves their odds of repayment.

By contrast, home loans historically required very minimal skin on behalf of the owner. No or low down-payments were required to secure a home loan. As we all know, a few years ago when the housing market turned just enough to eliminate the owner's exposure, owners simply walked away from their homes. This led to an escalation in mortgage foreclosures and a resulting economic downturn.

There is a clear correlation between the degree of ones negative exposure due to limited escape options and the probability of success. Consequently, if you are operating your business on a part-time basis while you hang on to your day-job, perhaps your day-job is preventing your part-time business from being all it can be.

Being all-in personally and financially certainly forces you to learn to overcome all obstacles and brings out the best in you. While I do not advocate quitting your day-job without a solid business plan and understanding of the market, once a success path is confirmed, being 100% committed will improve your odds of success through forced learning.

However, success is not guaranteed simply based on your commitment to the outcome. The market must be big enough and customers must be able to be stimulated to buy your product or service. That being said, with a solid business plan and by committing yourself 100% to the outcome by removing options for retreat, you can certainly amplify your probability of success.

*How committed are you to your business success?*

## Something Never Taught in an MBA Program

For the entrepreneur the division between personal and business life is virtually nonexistent. Running a small business requires a significant commitment of time and energy; time and energy that might otherwise be devoted to ones family and other interests, but is instead spent on the business.

If an entrepreneur has family members who underestimate the time and energy necessary to launch or sustain a business and make frequent demands on his or her time, it is likely that the entrepreneur will become overwhelmed and not succeed on either front.

*Do you have the level of family support necessary to succeed?*

## Learn To Supplement Your Income Before Taking The Plunge

Many would-be entrepreneurs think in terms of full-time employment, either from a job or through a business they own.

Eighty percent of businesses are considered non-employer businesses according the Small Business Administration (SBA). Many start out as part-time efforts. Some progress into full-time businesses with employees, but many are simply businesses designed to supplement the owner's income.

My first foray into the world of business came as a part-time franchise business when I considered myself to be under-employed. I learned a lot about how business worked while I still enjoyed a paycheck "working for the man". Only after I learned my business lessons did I consider starting a business which required me to quit my day job.

*Are you ready to practice being an entrepreneur?*

## *Who is Your Jester?*

Entrepreneurs often invest in products or new service offerings that are doomed to fail from the outset because they fail to notice what is apparent to a casual observer.

When we expect a particular outcome, or are intently focused on a specific measurement, we often can't see the obvious.

The human mind uses filters to allow it to focus. However, the things it filters are often important to understanding the problem.

In medieval times jesters were used to help monarchs see the obvious. The stars we see at night are out even during the day. We just can't see them because the sun is too bright.

*What are you missing that is right in front of you?*

## *Veterans Make Good Entrepreneurs*

A study performed by the Small Business Administration (SBA) shows that veterans are 45% more likely to become entrepreneurs then non-veterans.

One factor is that veterans have shown a propensity for risk taking by agreeing to fight and die if necessary.

When compared to veterans who retired after twenty years, veterans who leave after their first enlistment are the most likely to become entrepreneurs. Military retirees that remained on active duty after twenty years also showed a higher rate of entrepreneurship by about 7.5% for each additional year they continued to serve. This is likely due to the security afforded by a larger retirement check as well as their age.

The Kauffman Foundation reports that 55-64 years olds, regardless of military service, were 1/3 more likely to be entrepreneurial, which demonstrates that age and family situations may be a greater factor then just a larger military retirement check.

Among military retirees, Officers were more likely to be entrepreneurs then their enlisted counterparts, due to the fact that the officers had more formal education. This same correlation holds true in the general population. College-educated individuals are more entrepreneurial then non-college educated individuals.

*Do you know a vet who would make a good entrepreneur?*

## Business Ownership Changes the Entire Family

When I worked in a corporate job I worked very hard and often had to put in extra hours to complete projects. However, when I left the office, I pretty much left work behind. I had the time to coach soccer, go on vacations, and, overall, remain engaged in all aspects of the family. Family time was abundant and income was predictable and consistent.

As a business owner I was never off the clock. The thought of failure and losing everything we worked for was always on my mind. There were always issues that needed attention and subjects that needed more research or further contemplation. As a result, I was always preoccupied with the business.

Furthermore, as a business owner there never seemed to be any time to volunteer, go on vacation for more than three or four days, or help much in the raising of my kids or running of our household. The support I received from my family was critical to my success, and helped shape their lives as well. My wife was forced to pick up the slack in running our household and my kids had to become more self-sufficient.

*How engaged is your family in the success of your business?*

## A Lesson From The Ship Of Gold

Any business owner with investors can take a lesson from Gary Kindler's book "Ship of Gold". On the surface it is a historical account about finding the SS Central America, which sunk off the Carolina coast while carrying twenty-one tons of gold. However, if you look a little deeper, the story provides a valuable lesson for the entrepreneur. Essentially, the book demonstrates how value in a business is created.

Since it has been a while since I read the book I'm taking a few editorial liberties when it comes to costs, but I think you will get the point.

At first the treasure-hunters needed to raise some seed money to determine a general location of the shipwreck. Let's say they needed to raise one hundred thousand dollars to fund this first research phase. They sold one hundred thousand shares of stock at just one dollar per share, since the risk was very high at this point in the project.

After the research phase was complete the treasure-hunters had a pretty good idea of the general location of the wreck, but needed more money, say one million dollars, to rent a boat with a side-scan sonar they could drag along the ocean floor to look for anomalies. The project's risk was reduced as a result of the research phase, so this time they sold another one hundred thousand shares for ten dollars per share.

Once the money was raised for phase two and the boat hired, they discovered two anomalies that might be the wreck of the SS Central America. Now they needed to raise even more money, say ten million dollars, to rent a larger boat with a submersible sub to look over the anomaly, to see if it was the shipwreck, and bring the gold to the surface. As a result of the sonar test they further lowered the project's risk, and now sold one hundred thousand more shares of stock for one hundred dollars per share.

You get the picture; if you were a first round investor you paid one dollar for your share but a third round investor paid one hundred times that amount to own the same share. The treasure hunters did find the shipwreck, but the lesson to be learned is that even before the endeavor ever made any money from recovering the gold, the value of the enterprise rose as the probability of success improved.

A business "idea" has little value until a founder writes a business plan which creates the initial value. The first investor in gets the most value for the least amount of money since his investment represents the most risk. The second investor in pays more for his stock then the first investor since there is more value and less risk.

When it comes to raising equity capital to fund your venture, the price per share will vary depending upon the perceived level of project risk. The lower the risk of failure, the more the investor should pay for the stock.

Every stock transaction will carry a different level of risk and reward and should be priced accordingly. When you raise equity capital from new investors in your business the amount of ownership surrendered should be proportional to the risk/reward level at the time of your offering.

*How can you apply the lesson from the ship of gold to your next fund raising effort?*

## *Salary vs. Standard of Living*

Americans are fixated on how much they make. People use their salary as a report card of sorts to compare their success to others.

The problem is that income is often a poor measurement of success, since it is decoupled from a person's standard of living. It is not how much money you make, but what you can buy with that money that affects your standard of living.

A few years ago this point was hammered home for me when one of my boys moved from Colorado Springs, Colorado to Bentonville, Arkansas. The composite Consumer Price Index (CPI) in Bentonville is roughly two-thirds of the CPI in Colorado Springs. Therefore, my son can earn one-third less in salary while maintaining the same standard of living. Income does not translate directly to a person's standard of living. Something that became all to evident two years later when he moved back to Colorado Springs.

The same elements that go into CPI also affect a business. Real estate, utilities, healthcare and wages are all impacted by the location of the business.

A manufacturing client of mine is considering moving her business from Colorado Springs, Colorado to Pueblo, Colorado. A short forty mile move will allow her to take advantage of a twenty-five percent reduction in CPI.

*Does your business need to be located where it is currently, or can you improve your profit margins by moving your business to a nearby city with a lower CPI?*

## *Being an Inventor Does Not Make You an Entrepreneur*

Coming up with a great idea is the easy part. It is the execution of bringing your idea to market that is the hard part.

I have run into many clients who have a great idea, around which they want to build a business. When I mention that they can license the product to a manufacturer and get either a one-time lump sum payment or a royalty of say 2-10% for minimal risk, most say they would rather get a bigger share of the pie and build their own business around their invention.

However, starting up a manufacturing facility is not cheap or easy. It requires considerable skills that the fledgling entrepreneur most often does not have. Assuming they tackle the manufacturing facility, have a handle on quality control issues, and have properly priced their product, they generally have no distribution channel with which to get their product to the public.

Most retail stores prefer to work with large distributors with a huge catalog of products rather then thousands of small manufacturers.

Selling online means lots of shipping and handling costs, as well higher customer acquisition and logistics costs since there are no bulk orders. Spikes and lulls in sales create order fulfillment and carrying cost issues, and then there is customer support and return order processing.

Furthermore, you have to pay commissions if you sell through online stores. If someone rips off your idea you have to enforce your patent, which costs more money. In the end the inventor is often much better off inventing new stuff and selling their ideas or collecting royalties rather than trying to become an entrepreneur.

*Are you really an inventor who mistakenly thinks they want to become an entrepreneur?*

## *Do You Leverage Group Think?*

New government policies and news events affect group-thinking, which also creates sales opportunities. For example, recent talk of potential gun legislation caused a run on guns and ammo.

Movement, whether economic or emotional, creates opportunities for small businesses who can spot them and react more quickly then larger companies.

Savvy small business owners look at external events that will create movement in their industry, and take advantage of them.

Keeping your eyes and mind open to opportunities is free and can translate into business success.

*What recent events have taken place in your market that will impact your industry?*

*How will the media coverage of the MERS or ZIKA virus hitting our shores, climate change, or healthcare reform impact your business?*

## Take Baby Steps

Is the enormity of the business planning process keeping
you from launching your business idea out of fear of failure
or financial loss if you are not successful? If so, you are
not alone.

While a physical business plan will increase your odds of
success, it is the knowledge you gain in all facets of
business that will ultimately help you achieve success.

So how do you get this knowledge? Take baby steps. Evil
Knievel (the motorcycle daredevil) didn't start out jumping
over nineteen cars on his first attempt. He started with one
car, then two, and so on. Occasionally he crashed along the
way, learned from his mistakes, and attempted the jump
again. Eventually he built up to nineteen cars, a record he
held for twenty-seven years.

*How can you break down your business ambitions into
smaller baby steps?*

## *Buy Four Green Houses Before You Buy a Red Hotel*

The Wall Street Journal once printed an article that listed the five things an entrepreneur needs to build a successful business. The list was in the order of importance from most required to least.

1. Access to Capital
2. Business Acumen
3. Energy
4. Industry Knowledge
5. Idea

Most would-be entrepreneurs I see have some degree of the bottom three items (Energy, Industry Knowledge, and an Idea) but have little if any money or business acumen. So how does one get money and business acumen? Start small and build from there.

If your idea is to open a restaurant, why not open a mobile hotdog stand first, like the ones in front of Home Depot. That sort of business costs a lot less to start up, and if you manage to mess it up you'll learn some valuable lessons along the way without breaking the bank.

In addition to the knowledge you gained, if you're successful you might now have the start-up capital you need to open your restaurant.

Robert Kiyosaki, the author of "Rich Dad Poor Dad", discussed the value the game Monopoly had in his education when he wrote that "you buy four houses and trade them in for a red hotel." The message here is that you don't buy the hotel right out of the gate. You build up your knowledge so that when you can afford the red hotel you are more likely to be successful.

*Are you trying to buy the red hotel before you learned your lessons by owning four green houses?*

## Do You Have Access To Capital?

A wise man once told me "If you are successful you will need more money." He also said "If you are not successful you will need more money."

The undisputed leader in business failure is that businesses just run out of money before they become profitable. Access to capital is therefore the single biggest element entrepreneurs need to have lined up to give them the best hope of success.

Capital comes from one of two sources: Debt (loans) and Equity (investors/stock). Debt is hard to come by for startups without a long history, so equity financing is usually your only option. That being said, everyone knows people who might make good equity partners.

Do you know a successful or retired entrepreneur or a professional such as a doctor, lawyer, or CPA? These people make up seventy percent of all millionaires and may be looking for a private business in which to invest.

*Do you have access to sufficient capital?*

### Do You Have What It Takes To Be a Successful?

How do you know if you have what it takes to be a successful entrepreneur? While the answer to this question may have many facets, certainly one element to being successful is what I call "Valuing Goals over Sacrifice." So what does this really mean?

On a hunting trip with my son a while back we discussed a hunting strategy that involved getting up before sunrise and hiking across a muddy field on a freezing cold and foggy morning. It was one of those mornings where you just want to stay in bed, perhaps with a nice cup of coffee, rather than expose yourself to the raw elements. Clearly the chances of having a successful hunt this day were reduced dramatically by the weather.

It would be easy to convince yourself that the sacrifice just didn't justify the goal. If you are one to say "Since there is a limited opportunity for success, why should I expose myself to being miserable?", you are likely not yet ready to be an entrepreneur.

In the business world successful entrepreneurs tend to be individuals that are highly goal/effort-oriented. No amount of sacrifice or pain will deter them from their objectives to start or operate a business. Provided it is the best path, they will do whatever it takes to accomplish their objective.

Are you willing to get up early and make that cold call at 6:00am to a potential client, even though the chances of success are small?

Are you willing to speak to a professional group after hours, even though public speaking is a major fear of yours and the commitment requires working late into the evening?

The key here is that many successful entrepreneurs especially for innovation to technology based businesses choose the "best path" to their goal, not the easiest or shortest path. Goal-oriented entrepreneurs do not flinch at placing themselves in painful situations if they improve their odds of success even a little bit. The successful entrepreneur values the goal and is willing to sacrifice much to obtain it.

*Do you have what it takes to be a successful entrepreneur?*

## *Are You Committed?*

A few years ago I planted a garden for the first time in several years. The first few weeks were brutal. I visited the garden every day, looking for new plant shoots to confirm my skills as a gardener. I was constantly concerned over issues like was I watering too much or not enough, was the soil prepared properly, or was I using the right fertilizers and nutrients?

When the new shoots arrived so did the rabbits and deer, so we erected a fence to keep them out. With the watering on a timer and my plants safe from predators, I soon stopped visiting the garden every day. Over time I turned my attentions elsewhere, and for a while I lost my commitment to gardening.

In the dark reaches of my mind I must have concluded that if everything died or was eaten by animals I was not going to go hungry. While it was nice to grow my own vegetables, I was not committed to the outcome like my subsistence-based ancestors must have been. After all, I had options besides having a successful garden. I could shop for vegetables at a supermarket or eat out.

If my life depended upon the yield from my garden, I would have spent significantly more time researching gardening, and I would have become a pretty good gardener. However, since I had options, I was quick to abandon the garden when competing demands arose.

Since then I have reinvented my gardening hobby and with it my commitment to gardening. I no longer grow common vegetables I could purchase locally, but now grow exotic plants in a hydroponic garden, upping the technical difficulty to keep me challenged.

*How committed are you?*

*Do you having income from sources other then your business that diminish your business commitment and divert you from learning opportunities related to your business?*

*Is too much income security preventing you from building a business that is all it can be?*

## How to Leverage a Turning Tide

Three quarters of all firms in the United States are categorized as "non-employers". Non-employers are business that provide work for only a single or part-time owner.

While small businesses which employ many people are usually started in response to marketplace opportunities, non-employer business are often started as occupational decisions. They can be a way to deal with the loss of a job or serve as part-time ventures to supplement the owner's income when they are under-employed.

A study conducted by the SBA discovered that for every one "employer business" started there were three "non-employer business" started. When turnover, the ratio of entry to exit rates in business, was examined, turnover was closely associated with the amount of capital required to start the venture. Specifically, businesses with greater start-up capital requirements had lower turnover, while business with lower start-up requirements, like service-based business, had much higher turnover.

Another correlation related to regional unemployment rates. The study found that when the labor market worsens people respond by finding clients to work for rather than employers. By contrast, as the economy and labor market improves, many of the owners of non-employer, service-type businesses chose to close up their business in favor of full-time employment.

When a business closes it leaves their clients stranded, making these clients available to a new provider.  Some owners may elect to cherry-pick their best clients and continue to conduct business on a part-time basis while they take up employment.  For those that choose to remain in business, new market-driven opportunities will present themselves as clients accustomed to services are left without a provider.

Many of these providers, responding to the new market demand, will evolve from the ranks of the non-employer to become employer firms as they pick up these new clients. These new firms would be well-served to take the time now to develop a solid business plan so that they can take maximum advantage of any changing tide.

*Are you prepared to take advantage of a turning tide?*

## What an Ear of Corn Can Teach Us

If you were given an ear of corn today you would have a few options. You could eat the ear of corn and receive nourishment today. You could forgo the nourishment from the corn today and save/horde the ear for its seeds, which you could sell or plant at a later date. You could forgo the nourishment from the corn today and plant the seeds and have lots of corn plants with hundreds of ears of corn by this time next year. Or you could combine the options: eat some of the corn, save some of it, and wait and plant some.

The prevailing culture in American is one of instant gratification, which translates into our business culture. Most Americans if given the ear of corn would simply eat it. But how hard would it be to eat most of of the corn today and save just a few kernels so you could plant them next year?

On average, a single ear of corn has about 800 kernels. Would you really miss the nourishment from not eating a few of the seeds? After all, an investment of saving just a one seed from consumption could by next year grow an entire plant with multiple ears from each kernel you didn't eat today.

Many business owners leach every dollar of profit to support a consumption-oriented lifestyle for themselves today. They live in "daylight compartments" and consume all that their businesses produce. Life is good in the short term, since they ate their entire ear of corn. However, these businesses will soon become part of the statistics on business failure.

By contrast, a person who is willing to deny themselves the satisfaction of eating the entire ear of corn today, and start by just keeping a few kernels for seed stock to plant next year, will in only a year or two never be wanting for corn ever again. And it all started with saving just a few seeds from the first ear. Too many business owners do not make the needed investments in their businesses to allow them to grow.

*Are you guilty of taking too much from your business and not investing in its future?*

## Challenges of Creating a New Category

My first foray into the world of small business was with Invisible Fencing. At the time, in the early 1980's, it was a new product in a whole new category of electronic pet containment systems.

We were covered by a patent, so no other company could sell a product like ours. It used a transmitter to send a radio signal along a wire you ran around your yard, and a compact receiver on a pet's collar. The collar administered a tone and vibration, to be followed by a mild shock, if the pet didn't retreat from his position toward the center of the yard.

Millions of Americans owned dogs, the principal pet contained by the system, and the product made sense on so many levels. It had no maintenance, was scalable to very large properties with little additional cost, etc. No one else could sell a similar product, so competitive pricing was not a issue. A dream come true, right? Most people would agree. However, for me, it was not the case.

First, I have to admit I was new to the world of small business, and made lots of mistakes. The fact was I had to spend 99% of my time educating people about what an electronic fence was, as they often confused it with an electric fence. Invisible as it was, the word "invisible" also created a road block to selling, since many people dismissed it as a hoax. In the end, I learned that having a new and novel product like no other, while it may look very appealing from the inside, represents a business that will take lots of energy to get any traction at all.

As pointed out in the book "Techno Trends", by author Daniel Burrus, the fluorescent light took eighty-two years from invention to wide application. Even the ballpoint pen took over fifty years to gain any traction. If you think that having a great idea for a new product in a new category will bring you fame and fortune, guess again. New technologies takes time to reach the point where they pop.

*Do you have the financial resources to wait it out?*

## *Free SBA Tool to See How your Business Stacks Up*

It is important to periodically benchmark your business against others in your industry and/or in your local area.

A free tool that is offered by the SBA called "Size Up" can help.  Once you select your industry and location, you can enter data about your company and compare it with your peers to see how it stacks up.

You can compare your business in terms of revenue, time in business, employee wages, as well as many other factors.

You can get a map of your competition, your customers, your suppliers, and even drill down on customer expenditures.

You can even get a report on the best places to advertise.

*When was the last time you did an benchmark analysis on your business?*

## *Demand Curve Demographics*

Understanding consumer demographics is the key to making smart business decisions, and no one, to my knowledge, does a better job then Harry Dent.

It is no surprise to anyone that every time you use a credit card, debit card, loyalty card, etc. for a purchase, the UPC code and the credit card billing address can be used to track the purchase back to you. Based upon your census information your age, gender, and other key facts can be linked to the same purchase.

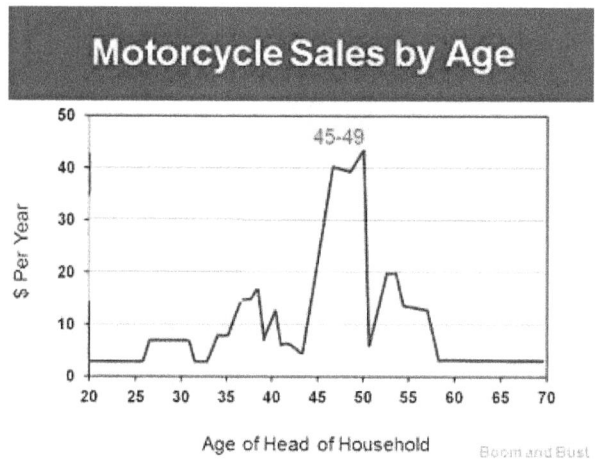

Harry Dent takes this large repository of data and codifies it to create what he calls "Demand Curves". The image above looks at motorcycle sales based on age. As you can see, there is huge spike in motorcycle sales between age 45

and 49.

Moreover, everyone is aware that there is a baby boomer generation currently aging in the US. This generation represents an over 20% increase in population over the generations before and after it, and it stands to reason that as this generation passed through the ages of 45-49 it generated a motorcycle buying bubble. This explained the recent rise in motorcycle sales and the growing fortunes of the likes of Harley Davidson.

Spending waves are pretty uniformly distributed by age. However, age dispersion can be different depending upon your location. For example, the median age in Boulder Colorado is 28.7 years old, compared to Boca Raton, Florida, where the median age is 45.7.

I included a copy of Harry Dent's Demand Curves PDF file in the resources tab of www.SteveBizBlog.com.

*How can you use your knowledge of demand curves to improve your business decisions?*

## *What We Can Learn From The Texas Cattle Industry.*

Longhorn Cattle were introduced to the the Americas by the Spanish between the 16th and 18th centuries. The cattle industry back then was primarily a small-scale industry. Beef was not very popular, so cattle were raised primarily for the value of their hides.

Because there was no refrigeration, any cattle used for beef had to be delivered on the hoof to cities where the beef was to be consumed.

The first cattle drives from Texas were to supply beef to San Francisco during the gold rush of the 1850s. The journey took over 6 months but proved to be profitable, since cattle that cost $5 to $10 in Texas were worth $20 in San Francisco.

During the first half of the1860's, demand for beef and leather during the civil war decimated the cattle industry in every state except for Texas, where the Longhorn continued to thrive. The nation's economy was in ruins after the civil war, but Texas had over five million head of cattle.

Unfortunately, there was no easy way to get the cattle to major population centers. That all changed with the introduction of the transcontinental railroad, which was completed in 1869. With the advent of the railroad, cattle could be loaded on rail-cars and transported thousands of miles to virtually any city in the US.

The era of the cowboy was born. Cattle drives from Texas followed the Goodnight-Loving, Western, Chisholm, or Shawnee trails to cities along the new transcontinental railroad. With the new-found wealth derived from the cattle industry, cities along the route prospered.

These cities spawned support industries catering to the consumption of liquor, gambling, prostitution, and even the need for peace officers. But as the cattle industry grew, it attracted more and more people wanting to make their fortunes.

Soon cattle became abundantly available, resulting in a dramatic drop in the price of beef, ultimately wiping out many an entrepreneurs' hopes of cashing in on the new cattle industry.

In business today this same history is repeated over and over again. The phenomenon is sometimes referred to as a "Bubble". A new industry is established, then sits and simmers until several seemingly unrelated events come together. Then the market explodes. Huge profits are made by the entrepreneur that can spot the trend early and be in a position to take advantage of it. As more and more people wanting their piece of the pie enter the market and overproduce the product, they eventually drive down profits, driving out all but most efficient businesses.

Savvy entrepreneurs understand when to get in, how to become cost-effective, and when to get out.

*How does the history of the cattle industry apply to your current or next business venture?*

## *Ignorance Can Be Bliss*

It's great to be highly familiar with the industry in which you plan to compete, but many times insiders see too many challenges and obstacles and never start a new business.

Entrepreneurs with limited industry knowledge sometimes see opportunities because the industry has changed in ways that more well-established players are blinded to. Serious entrepreneurs trust their ability to beat a new path to the opportunity.

*Are you too knowledgeable about your industry to see new opportunities?*

## *The Curse of Knowledge*

The curse of knowledge prevents us from seeing the world as our customers see it. To demonstrate this curse, try this experiment with a friend. Think of popular song like "Jingle Bells" or "Happy Birthday." Then tap out the melody for your friend and ask him or her to try to guess what song it is.

From the sender's point of view, the melody is playing in their head as they tap out the tune. In clinical tests, if asked to bet on the probability that their friend would correctly identify the tune, about ½ said the other party would recognize it.

However, from the listener's prospective, the tapping sounds only like Morse Code. In fact, only about 2% of the listeners were able to correctly identify the tune. The fact that the sender thought the listener would identify the melody 1 out of every 2 times while it was actually closer to 1 in 50 is the curse of knowledge.

An often cited example of the curse of knowledge is encapsulated in the story of a hardware store that sells drill bits. The salesperson is burdened with the curse of knowledge and thinks he is selling drills. However, the customer is actually buying the holes that the drill makes so he can hang a family picture.

In business, we have knowledge that the customer does not

have. No matter how hard we try, we can't unring the knowledge bell. Therefore, there is an imperative for businesses to test assumptions with real customers prior to going through the expense of development and implementation of ideas.

I remember a case when I worked for Digital Equipment Company. We wrote a manual about how to unpack and install a new printer. One of the steps was to uncage the printer head, which was secured only for shipping purposes. Since the printer was considered user installable, we gave the new printer and the manual to a secretary. We asked her to follow the instructions and install the printer. When it came to the step about uncaging the printer head, the manual said, "Cut the tie-wrap that holds the printer head in place for shipping." Unfortunately, she was not familiar with what a tie-wrap was and we watched in horror as she cut the data cable that connected the printer head to the printer's circuits. As writers we had assumed everyone understood what a tie-wrap was because we suffered from the curse of knowledge.

One technique used in businesses to expose and overcome the curse of knowledge is to employ the "3 Whys" technique. By repeatedly subjecting your answer to the question "why?" you can often get to the core of the matter and see what the customer sees.

Here is how it might work in practice.

1. "I sell drills." Why?
2. "So customers can drill holes." Why?
3. "So they can insert a molly into the hole." Why?
4. "So they can hang a picture."

In the end, the salesman is not selling drills, but a tool to help the customer hang his picture. While this might be a simple example, often the customer has no idea they need a drill. They just know they have a problem; they want to hang a picture and they need a hole in order to do that.

*Do your solutions and answers suffer from the curse of knowledge?*

## Rise of the Micro Business

Each month I sit on a panel at the US Air Force Academy where solderers, sailors and airman are preparing for life as civilians. Around the room are flip chart pages that list the things these separating officers and enlisted folks want from their future employment. Always near the top of the list is job security.

My father worked for the same employer for most of his adult life. Well, that simply is not the case in today's world. The underpinning of income risk from a single job has changed. No longer is a job with a employer the most risk-free way to earn a living. The job security landscape has changed. Today, corporate jobs are often more risky then being self employed in a micro business.

Micro businesses often have many customers. When one of the customers falls on hard times and is forced to terminate their contract, the micro business has other customers that can often pick up the slack.

While many people have become rich by focusing their investments on a single business or stock, such actions are considered risky in the world of investing. Financial advisers recommend that rather then concentrating your investments in one area, you diversify your portfolio to reduce risk. This same philosophy holds true for income sources.

Having many smaller income streams is much less risky then getting all your income from a single source, your job.

*What is your level of income risk?*

## *Number One Stated Reason For Not Starting a Business*

By far the most common feedback I get from would-be entrepreneurs for not moving forward is related to their fear of failure and not being able to provide for their family.

The traditional concept of a person quitting their day job to start a business is no longer valid. I think this concept remains pervasive in many people's minds because potential entrepreneurs are consumers themselves.

They see brick and mortar establishments that requires a large upfront investment and full-time commitments, and think that's what it takes to run a business. Today that is just not the case, as most businesses are virtual businesses run out of a spare bedroom in a home. More and more businesses are started as a part-time endeavors that grow into full-time jobs over time.

*Are you suppressing your entrepreneurial urges based on old school start-up thinking?*

## A Great Idea Is Not Enough

Nikola Tesla was perhaps one of world's greatest inventors. His experiments with alternating current or AC proved that transmitting electricity through copper wire with AC was much more efficient than using direct current or DC, the power source used by Thomas Edison.

He also invented the electric motor and even invented wireless radio, which were inventions that changed the world.

Unfortunately Nikola Tesla had no social skills or business skills, which prevented his success. In contrast, George Westinghouse and Guglielmo Marconi, who were much better businessmen, capitalized on Nikola Tesla's inventions and made fortunes while Nikola Tesla died penniless.

To become a successful entrepreneur requires much more then a great mind for inventions, it requires business acumen.

*What are you doing to improve your nose for business?*

## Testing the Market

Sometimes you run across a unique product that you think you might be able to sell on the internet, or you have an idea for a new piece of software but it is not developed yet, and you would like to know if the product will sell before you make an investment. In such cases you want to employ a three page website to test the market's readiness.

On the landing page you place the description of the product with all the elements that would make your customer want to buy, including an "Order" button. When they select the order button you collect their payment information. This makes sure they are willing to exchange money for your product. Then, when they hit the "Submit Order" button, you bring up the 3rd page that indicates that you have sold out of V1.0 and will be shipping V2.0 in 30 days at no extra charge, and offer a refund if the wait is not acceptable.

This gives you 30 days to either secure the item or develop the software. This technique was used successfully by a piano teacher that had developed a basic tool to schedule his appointments with students, and suspected that other music teachers might have the same need. But before going through the trouble of developing a more formal product and running the risk it might not be accepted, he used the three page website to see if others had a similar need and were willing to pay for the scheduling solution he had envisioned.

It turned out that others had the same issues, and he developed the tool to great success.

*Can you employ a three page website to test out your next idea?*

## Diversify Your Small Business Risk

Most people I talk to about investments believe in having a diversified portfolio vs. consolidating all their assets in one company as a way to mitigate their risk. However, these same people go all-in on much more risky small business ideas with no partners.

Entrepreneurs understand the value of shared risk and reward programs. As a oil and gas investor, many drilling companies, with what they truly believe is a good prospect, reach out to other similar oil companies for fractional investments in the prospect to share the risk and reward. In this way they achieve much greater diversification with the same amount of invested capital, and even get a collective brain trust to review the prospect based on each partner's experience. If one partner loves the idea but no one else does, it is likely a bad deal.

*Do you share risk and reward with business partners when it comes to business?*

## *How to Choose the Right Occupation*

The vast majority of people work solely for the purpose of making money to support their lifestyle. Unfortunately, this often leads to choosing occupations that do not provide much in the way of personal fulfillment.

When you do not get any type of personal fulfillment from your work, going to work becomes a chore that you avoid whenever possible. By contrast, if your work is personally fulfilling, it will not feel like work. You will wake up each morning and look forward to going to work, and ultimately will devote more of your energy to your occupation.

For most people the narrative is you need to work hard for your economic survival and you are grateful just to have a job. Successful entrepreneurs conduct extensive introspective soul searching to discover what they love to do and match it to their talents, what the world needs, and what can earn them money.

The diagram above is a great tool that provides a more

visual depiction of how to locate that ideal business that is your sweet spot.

*Do you get personal fulfillment from your work?*

## *Tacit vs. Explicit Knowledge*

The other day my son got a new phone and was demonstrating its native voice recognition software. The phone, which uses the Google engine, could answer some questions such as, "What is tomorrows forecast?" without him ever removing the phone from his pocket. However, his demonstration ran into problems locating answers to other questions such as, "How do you drive a car?" Being a teachable moment, I began to explain to him the difference between explicit and tacit knowledge.

One of the problems with obtaining any kind of knowledge is that while some kinds of knowledge can be easily codified and articulated to others, there are also some forms of knowledge that are much harder to pass on. For example, a non-fiction book is a good example of capturing and sharing what is known as explicit knowledge. While I can read a book or watch a video to learn to play better golf, which would be considered explicit knowledge, there is not substitution for actually playing golf to take that explicit knowledge to the next level.

Explaining how to ride a bike can only go so far. To truly ride a bike requires knowledge you can really only obtain by trying to ride a bike.

When I gave up riding motocross bikes for a street bike many years ago, I had to take a written test to get my motorcycle endorsement. In the study materials, they attempted to convey a piece of information which made no sense to someone without some degree of tacit knowledge. The manual said "to make a right turn, turn the handle bars to the left." When I read it, I was sure it was a typo. I had rode bikes for years and was sure I turned right to go right.

Defiantly, I dropped the manual, hoped on my bike, and tried it. Sure enough, they were right. We all had been turning left to steer the bike to the right ever since learning to ride a 2-wheeler bicycle, but we never could have explained the action to others in a way that would have made sense to them.

You can take all the business courses on the planet to learn how to start and run a business, but nothing substitutes for actual experience. I often tell people to fail small. I can tell you how to write a business plan, how to do market research, or how to perform basic accounting skills which is explicit in nature. I would have a much more difficult time trying to explain how to identify new business opportunities, explain which local resources are best for you, or how to deal with business uncertainty.

Before embarking on a new business, I often tell clients with no business experience to first try starting a really simple business that does not cost them much if it fails. The tacit lessons they will learn is knowledge that you can only learn by actually trying.

*How do you gain your tacit knowledge?*

## *Belief vs. Assumption*

An "assumption" is where you believe something to be true, but it is yet unproven while a "belief" is something you are certain is true. However, our beliefs may in fact be assumptions that are in the end false.

To understand this concept, we can start with our mindset. Our mindset effects the choices we make which in turn leads to the actions we take and the outcomes we experience. The outcomes we experience can then either modify our mindset, creating a new assumption, or the evidence can be ignored because of our belief system.

For example, a young boy's mindset may be based on the assumption that all dogs are friendly since he has only experienced friendly dogs. So he makes the choice to pet a passing dog. The action of leaning over to pet the dog startles the dog and the outcome is that the dog snaps at his hand. The boy's new mindset is modified from "all dogs are friendly" to "not all dogs are friendly." The boy created a new assumption based on the outcome and his experience.

Sometimes, however, our mindset is defined by our beliefs and are based on incorrect information. In this situation, we find ways to reinforce our incorrect mindset. For example, until only recently, the collective belief was that the world was flat. The belief colored your observations.

While standing on the beach, you watched a boat sail out of

the harbor. As the boat approached the horizon, it got smaller and then disappeared. You attributed the disappearance of the boat to the commonly held belief that the world was flat and the ship just sailed off the end of the world, reinforcing your belief.

However, as we know today, this belief, while commonly held, was in fact false. Our belief system blinded us to the fact that in the afternoon the boat somehow returned. While inconvenient, the fact that the boat returned was ignored since it didn't fit our belief.

A common belief that keeps many people on the side lines when thinking about starting a small business is the belief that that entrepreneurs are innovators or that entrepreneurs are highly educated. Some are, but many are not.

Recognizing the difference between an assumption and a belief can open up your mind to new opportunities. Mark Twain once said,

> *"It ain't what you don't know that gets you into trouble... it's what you know for sure that just ain't so."*

So the lesson in business is you should always challenge beliefs and treat them as assumptions because your beliefs may not be facts.

*What beliefs do you take for granted that may not be true?*

## A Source of Innovation

Sometimes the best ideas come from just looking at another industry and applying their lessons to your business. For example, when Henry Ford visited a meat packing plant, he saw how a side of beef was placed on a trolley and as it traveled down a track, a line of butchers each performing a single task dismember the carcass into various cuts of meat for packaging.

This visit inspired him to reverse the process of removing parts and consider how it might be used to assemble parts. The conveyor driven assembly plant was born.

Prior to implementing the conveyor assembly system, when a craftsman built a car, it took more than 12 hours to assemble. However, after the conveyor assembly line process was implemented, it look just 1.5 hours.

Efficiency became a religion and soon the plant was turning out 1,000 cars per day. The skills required to build a car were engineered out of a process and became so simple any able-bodied man could perform a single receptive task with minimal education.

*What industry might hold the answers to your next innovation?*

## *Primary vs. Secondary Employers*

An important distinction to be made, which has significant implications to a city's ecosystems, is the distinction between primary and secondary employers.

Primary employers are industries that produce more goods and/or services than can be consumed by the local economy and therefore export a significant portion of them.

City officials and many investors focus their attention on primary employers because the revenue they produce comes from external sources and are infused into the local economy. The new money then has a significant impact on employment and wages in the local economy.

Much public time, money, and energy are expended in attracting and growing primary employers. For example, a manufacturing company is considered a primary employer and this is the reason why governments want to so desperately hold on to manufacturing jobs. Primary employers attract outside money. When the employer is paid for the products or services and new money flows in, he redistributes that wealth locally through wages paid to employees, and through products and services bought from local suppliers.

Secondary employers are those businesses that serve the local community and essentially recirculate local dollars. An example of a secondary employer is a restaurant which caters primarily to a local consumer market. While secondary employers play a significant role in the local economy by providing goods and services to residents and primary employers and even can create some level of gravity to attract primary employers to a community, they are often overlooked by government officials and ecosystem planners since they themselves do not directly attract new money to the community.

In a community ecosystem, when a business or person buys a product or service that was not produced locally, the money leaves the community. When you buy a product produced locally, buy a service delivered locally, or you produce a product or service that is consumed locally, you are simply recirculating money through the local economy. However, when you produce a product or provide a service that is consumed elsewhere, new money flows into the local economy.

You can think of a primary employer as focusing on the revenue portion of the ecosystem's P&L while the secondary employer is focused on keeping the expenses portion of the ecosystems P&L low so the community can profit. At the very least, a balance needs to be struck between money coming in and money going out.

If more money is exiting the local ecosystems, the community will eventually decay. However, if more money is flowing in than leaving, the community will grow and prosper. Hence the reason many cities have economic development centers and look to economic gardening programs to bring in or grow primary employers.

However, if you are a secondary employer, while considered vital to a local ecosystem because you keep the money from leaving the ecosystem, you are often treated like a second class citizen when it comes to services being offered by local government and small business support organizations. While both primary and secondary employers are vital to the local ecosystem, if you are contemplating a new business or operating one today, recognize that you might experience different treatment based on being either a primary or secondary employer.

*Are you a primary employer looking for ways to bring more money into your local ecosystems or are you a secondary employer more concerned with keeping the money from leaving your local ecosystem?*

## *Don't Be a Gold Digger*

I live in the Pikes Peak region and when this area was first settled, it was for the want of gold. Most came to seek their fortunes in the risky business of being a prospectors. The prospector's work was hard and while a few went on to earn their fortune, most barely scratched out a living as a laborer in the mines.

However, the most successful entrepreneurs were not the mining claim owners, but the main street business owners that opened the saloons, mercantile, restaurants, or brothels which took the earnings from the prospectors and the wages of the miners. The main street businesses had near zero financial risk, an abundance of eager customers, and didn't expose the owner's to the extremes of the elements.

Many entrepreneurs today are lured by the possibility of extreme riches of a new innovation or technology home run, but many will strike out in their pursuit to become a primary employer like the prospector. The secondary employer with their main street business may not hit that home run, but will be hitting singles and doubles all day.

*Are your business ambitions that of the risky prospector or are they that of the less risky main street businessman?*

## Four Questions Before You Start Something New

There are four questions that ever product or service company needs to ask before it embarks on a new business or product line.

1. Do customers recognize they have a problem?
2. If there was a solution to their problem, would they buy it?
3. Would they buy it from us?
4. Can we build it?

When I owned an Invisible Fencing dealership, my customers were quick to identify the problem of containing their dog. However, the additional maintenance issues such as painting, repairs, and weed whacking caused by installing a traditional stockade or chain link fence were never considered. While the buried wire used in an invisible fencing solution solved all these maintenance issues, the customer was not thinking beyond the initial problem and sales were initially very slow.

When you have a new product or service, customers often have a hard time recognizing the full extent of the problem which places a premium on customer education.

While our Invisible Fencing patent gave us exclusivity to the technology, it exacerbated the problem of "problem recognition" for our customers since Invisible Fencing dealers were the only ones getting the word out about our product. Once we got a customer's attention and showed them how it worked and they saw that it cost half the cost of the alternatives they were sold.

*Do you ask the right questions about your market when planning for a new product or service?*

## The Drug Dealer's Mindset

As a business coach, one of the single most common issues I see with new entrepreneurs is their lack of understanding of gross profit, gross margin, and the impact of operating expenses. Their focus is almost always exclusively on the revenue gained from sales. I often refer to this as the "drug dealer's mindset."

Petty street level drug dealers are often fronted a bunch of product they are expected to sell for the distributor. As they sell their product, they are left with a fist full of cash, making the drug dealer feel rich and leading them to believe that being a drug dealer is great gig. Unfortunately, what the drug dealer has in his hands is called revenue.

Revenue is the result of sales and is not what makes you rich. A business needs to subtract their cost of goods sold (COGS) from their revenue to equal their gross profit. Gross profit is what is used to pay operating expenses, including wages. The ratio of gross profit to revenue is known as gross margin. Gross margin is a much more important measurement of a business's health than revenue.

The drug dealer sees the cash generated from his sales, but forgets that much of the cash is not his. From that cash, he still owes the distributor the cost for the product he was initially fronted or he risks "getting fitted for a pair of cement overshoes," as my dad would say. What the drug dealer is left with after paying his distributor is gross profit.

Gross profit is what he can use to cover any expenses and pay himself for his efforts.

According to a study by the National Bureau of Economic Research, the typical petty drug dealer's average wage is only $6.00-11.00 per hour and many earn far less.

Many books on small business say that businesses live and die based on making sales. However, this is very misleading statement. Small businesses live and die based on their gross profit not from sales. After all, I can always make sales if I sell my product or service for less than my actual cost.

Even big businesses struggle with this distinction. My documentations and training business was acquired by a publicly held company during the dot-com era for our revenue alone. It was not bought for our gross profits, gross margins, or even the free cash we could provide. In fact, after the acquisition of my business, their business model doubled down on the "revenue only" drug dealer mindset.

After we were acquired we got new customers by agreeing to charge them less than their internal costs. We did this even if it meant our reduced price resulted in a tiny gross margin that would come no where close to covering even a small fraction of our operating expenses resulting in us losing money. We only offered this reduced price if the customers agreed to outsource their entire departments work to our company.

Since we were essentially giving away our services in the name of growing sales, it was no surprise that the division I managed grew from eight to thirty two million dollars in sales in only eighteen months.

Successful entrepreneurs know that it is not revenue or sales that count, but the gross margin you can produce from your sales. Without a healthy gross margin, your sales will not produce enough gross profit to cover your operating expenses and return a profit to the owners.

*Do you suffer from the drug dealer's mindset and think only about growing sales or are your focused on how much gross margin your sales will produce?*

## Your Best Chance to Succeed in Small Business

The other day I was asked if a person's idea would make a good business. Unfortunately, I had to tell them that it would not be a good idea for them to pursue. While the idea might have been a novel and successful venture in the right hands, they didn't have access to the level of capital it would require to make the business a success.

I'm often frustrated because I have to give this message over and over again to counteract the misconception that to be successful you need to have a new idea or invention. In fact, I'm sure I could write a book on assumptions that people have about business that are just not good advice. If you want to be a successful entrepreneur, I often recommend three things.

1. Choose a well established and perhaps antiquated industry. This is a direct contradiction to most people's thinking that the business needs to be in a new industry no one has thought of yet.

   The unfortunate reality, as I learned with my Invisible Fencing business, is that a business based on a new technology or service requires that you educate the customer, an extraordinarily expensive undertaking.

Unless you have access to a huge pool of investment capital, you are best served staying with a product or service people know and understand.

2. Pick an industry that relies on old technology or old thinking. When a new idea for a product or service is introduced, lots of companies try to compete for the customer mind share and educate the masses. As a few leaders begin to emerge, they acquire some of their competitors and the leadership that was initially responsible for the innovation is replaced by managers.

   The innovative leader is replaced by managers whose primary goal is to segment and organize the business into departments so it can become more efficient. However, when efficiency rises, it is at the expense of creativity. Over time these businesses grow and create internal systems that make it impossible to adopt new technology.

   For example, IBM was a mainframe company and built its system around the sale and service of mainframe computers. When the mini-computer came about, IBM could not make the shift without cannibalizing this revenue engine and Digital Equipment Corporation (DEC) emerged as the mini-computer leader. When the personal computer came about, DEC could not make the shift without cannibalizing its revenue engine, making Microsoft and Intel the next set of leaders.

3.  Find a unexploited niche where you can charge a
    premium based on your value to create a business
    with higher gross margins.

Rather than subscribe to the thinking "I need a brand new
technology or service to make a successful business," you
will have substantially less risk and a higher probability of
success if you look at starting a business in a well
established industry that has lived through consolidation.
These businesses are focused on efficiency and as a result
are less creative. However, you can exploit a niche that the
big players are ill prepared to capitalize on.

Still not convinced? Look at the make up of Inc 500
companies.

*Do you still subscribe to the the narrative that to create a
successful business you have to have a unique product or
service or are you focused on looking for ways to exploit
niche markets in well establishes industries?*

## *Value of Due Diligence*

The other day I had a client look at buying someone's business. The seller was very anxious to close the deal quickly which was the first indication that there might be a problem.

Looking at the finances for the prior three years, revenue and profits were definitely moving in the right direction and the buyer was eager to ink the deal, fearing that someone else would beat them to the punch. I urged the client to complete his due diligence before committing to the deal.

Fortunately, the client took my advise. In the subsequent due diligence, he later discovered that the seller had a very low reorder rate, signaling that the seller's product was not that well received. Further, we discovered that the seller was experiencing high employee turn over, perhaps indicating they didn't pay enough for the work they expected from their employees. Finally, we noticed that their customer acquisition costs were rising and their gross margins were shrinking.

While I often tell clients looking at buying someone else's business that the deal has to make sense financially, you also have to make sure you complete your due diligence and analyze all aspects of the business.

*Do you do your due diligence before you make a purchase?*

## Funding Plan

Most businesses require some form of funding to get started. A product company goes through 5 stages to get its product to market.

1. Idea
2. Proof of Concept
3. Product Design
4. Product Development
5. Manufacturing and Distribution

With each stage the chance of success increases, but so too do the capital requirements. While some businesses can progress through some or all the stages simply through "bootstrapping", and thereby preserve equity and maintain full control, many others will require other sources of financing.

The founder, followed closely by friends and family, are the most appropriate sources of financing to reach the Proof of Concept stage. With a Proof of Concept in hand, the entrepreneur needing additional capital may be able to engage an Angel Investor or an Angel Group to help fund the Product Design and Product Development stages.

If additional funds are still required in the Product Development and Manufacturing and Distribution stages, Venture Capital funds may be available, but these are generally not available until the Product Design stage is complete.

Finally, capital requirements for operations in the form of Manufacturing and Distribution costs may allow the entrepreneur to cross the chasm from equity financing to the realm of debt financing, and be funded through loans or through the issuing of bonds.

*What is your funding plan?*

## Retirement Account Funds New Business

Many would-be entrepreneurs have money tied up in retirement plans like IRAs or 401ks that could be used to fund their businesses. Many simply believe they can't access these funds until they reach the age of 59.5 without being subject to a premature distribution penalty. That being said, there are a few ways that you can fund your small business that do not require you to be subject to a premature distribution penalty. You can even retain retirement account tax advantages.

Most new entrepreneurs consider debt financing (bank loans) to be the number one funding source, since this is how most of us buy cars and homes. They soon discover that a more common source of funding for a start-up is equity financing (selling stock).

New entrepreneurs rarely grasp the concept of smart money investors. They fear outside investors will impact the direction of the company in a negative way, and often avoid giving away equity and control to others at all costs.

As is always good financial advice when cash flow lags an investment, as is the case when you are starting a new business, an equity infusion that pays the investment out of profits works best. This is because a new business often can't withstand fixed monthly debt payments, as their cash flow may be inconsistent or non-existent.

More mature businesses that have existing cash flow may take advantage of a debt infusion; one that pays principle and interest payments to the investor/lender from day one, and preserves equity and control.

In the next two articles we will look at how a self-directed IRA can be used for equity investments and how borrowing short-term funds from your own 401k can provide you the necessary cash for your business needs.

*Would your business benefit from having access to capital from your existing retirement account?*

## Using a Self-Directed IRA to Fund Your Business

Retirement accounts qualify for special tax treatment by the IRS. One of the most common retirement accounts is an IRA, where pretax dollars are deposited into an account and allowed to grow tax deferred. These funds are designed to create income during retirement and are subject to premature distribution penalties if the funds are used before the age of 59.5, except in specific situations.

The custodians of a typical IRA limit investments to public stocks, bonds, and mutual funds. By transferring a traditional IRA into a self-directed IRA, the IRA owner can invest in a much broader range of private placement opportunities. These include real estate and private businesses, as well as the investment categories of the traditional IRA.

The self-directed IRA is subject to the same tax rules as a traditional IRA, but is subject to a few restrictions. First, the self-directed IRA cannot hold assets in an S-corp, since an S-corp is restricted to individuals and trusts only. Next, while friends, employees, and other non-linear family members can be investors, the founder's parents, children, or spouse are considered prohibited transactions. They are not able to be investors using a self-directed IRA. This does not prohibit the founder or other family members, such siblings, aunts, uncles, cousins, etc., from being

Page 88

investors.

Finally, the founder can't be a key employee and a key investor at the same time. Therefore, the founder can't have a controlling interest or own more then 50% of the business. In essence the IRS wants to make sure your employment is controlled by others, and that you are not self-dealing from your IRA in such a way as to move retirement funds to your business in a way which can be used to fund immediate payments to you, such as through your salary.

You should seek specific advice from your CPA or a firm that specializes in these types of transactions before using a self-directed IRA to fund your business.

*Can your business benefit from investments from a self-directed IRA?*

## Using a 401k Loan to Fund Your Business

Retirement accounts qualify for special tax treatment by the IRS. A common retirement account is a 401k, where pretax dollars from you, which are often matched by your employer, are deposited into an account and allowed to grow tax deferred. These funds are designed to create income during retirement and are subject to premature distribution penalties if the funds are used before the age of 59.5, except in specific situations.

Borrowing from a 401k should not be taken lightly, but if you truly believe in your business plan and think there is a very good chance of a better than market return from investing in your own private business, then this might be right for you.

Receiving a loan from your 401k is not a taxable event unless the repayment rules are violated. Generally, you can borrow from your own account up to 50% of the account's value.

Since the principal is yours the loan payment and any interest assigned is paid back to your own 401k account. In this way, the transaction is like simply moving money from one pocket to another. As such, the cost of a 401k loan is less than the cost of paying real interest to a bank or other lending institution.

The repayment amortization for a 401k loan can not exceed

60 months and you can repay the loan early with no pre-payment penalty.

Other than an origination fee there are no costs when borrowing from your 401k. However, the borrowed funds are no longer available for investments inside the plan, so your 401k will grow more slowly as there is less principal at work.

Since loan payments are made with after-tax dollars there is a double taxation issue that applies to the interest portion of the repayment, but this is generally fairly small and outweighed by other factors.

If you fail to meet the repayment rules the loan can become a taxable event and subject you to premature distribution penalties.

You should seek specific advice from your CPA or your 401k custodian before using a 401k loan to fund your business.

*Can your business benefit from investments from a short-term loan from your 401k?*

### Get Your Private Employer to Pay Your Start-up Costs

In the last article we discussed using a loan from your 401k plan to fund your start up. With a 401k plan the employer often provides a match to the employee's contribution.

Both IRAs and 401k plans are consider defined contribution plans, meaning the contributions are fixed, but the returns are based on the returns from the investments made. This is in contrast to fixed annuities, such as social security and government retirement benefits, which are known as defined benefit plans. In these plans, the return is guaranteed and the contribution is not.

If your employer offers a defined contribution plan with a match it is a no-brainer to take advantage of the employer's generosity if you can afford the short term cash flow hit.

Before you launch your start-up, contribute as much as you can to maximize your employer's 401k match. Assuming your employer matched you dollar for dollar to a defined maximum, when the value of the 401k exceeds at least two times the funds you estimate necessary to start your business, you can set up a 401k loan.

Since you can borrow up to fifty percent of the value of a 401k plan and pay back the principal and interest on the loan to yourself, you have essentially gotten your employer to pay your start-up costs.

*Does your employer offer a 401k plan?*

*Do you have desire to own your own business someday?*

*If so, why not get your current employer to pay your start-up costs?*

# Cash Flow Quadrant

Robert Kiyosaki, the author of Rich Dad Poor Dad, uses a model he calls the Cash Flow Quadrant to explain the different ways income is generated. The next few articles we will look at how income is generated in each of the four quadrants.

Of course income can be earned from a single quadrant or from a combination of quadrants, but we will look at each quadrant separately in the following articles. The four quadrants are named E, S, B, and I. E stands for Employee, S for Self-Employed, B for Business Owner, and I for Investor.

If you divide the quadrant of income generation in half vertically, the left side contains quadrants E and S: Employee and Self-Employed. Here, your income is considered active income. That is, for the quadrants on the left side, you get paid for the number of hours you work. The two quadrants on the left are the playing field of the poor and the middle class.

On the right side of the quadrant are Business Owner and Investor, where your income is considered passive income. This means that you earn income from the labors of others. The two quadrants on the right are the playing field of the rich and financially independent.

Moving from the left side to the right requires capital, education, and a new mindset.

*What side of the quadrant do you want to earn your income from?*

## Employee – Cash Flow Quadrant

When you are an Employee you know you will get a paycheck as long as you continue to work for the business, even if the business is not profitable.

Earning a consistent wage each month is important when it comes to paying off debt, like home or car loans. However, full-time employees get their income from this single source, their job, and if they lose their job they lose 100% of their income.

They have to rely on unemployment to bridge any employment gaps. Moreover, in terms of taxes, employees pay the highest percentage of their income. The more you earn as an employee the higher your tax bracket, and you have no options to reduce your income through deductions or tax credits. Most Americans get their income from this quadrant.

*How much of your income comes from wages earned as a employee?*

## Self-Employed – Cash Flow Quadrant

When you are Self-Employed, you own a job. The government also refers to this group as non-employer businesses, where the owner is the only employee.

When you are self-employed you trade one boss for several bosses, known as your customers. While you have the flexibility to work the hours you want, you get paid only when you are under contract. The more you work, the more you get paid. There are no paid vacations or holidays for the self-employed.

Some self-employed individuals will derive income from several concurrent contracts, thereby achieving some level of diversification in their income. However, many self-employed workers simply work for a previous employer or for a single customer as a contractor, and do not achieve any income diversification. In fact, many self-employed individuals have undertaken more income risk by becoming self-employed, with little if any additional compensation.

In terms of taxes, the self-employed person will have to pay the employer portion of FICA in addition to the employee portion, which is known as the self-employment tax on all taxable income. However, many business expenses such as cell phones, travel, etc. can be paid for using pre-tax dollars, providing the self-employed opportunities to reduce their taxable income.

Savvy self-employed individuals price their services to adequately cover all their indirect expenses, including the additional employer-paid FICA share as well as any down-time experienced between projects.

*How much of your income comes from self-employment, and is it priced properly?*

## Business Owner – Cash Flow Quadrant

Being a Business Owner is different from being self-employed in that as a business owner you hire employees to do the work. That is not to say that the business owner does not work in the business also, but it means that they are getting paid for their effort as an employee in the business PLUS for being an investor in the business.

Business owners can scale up their business, which is not possible for the self-employed. As the business hires more and more employees a fraction of each employee's bill-rate is the owner's return on investment for the start-up capital, as well as for undertaking the additional risk of business ownership.

As the business grows it generates more and more wealth for the owner. Like being self-employed, as a business owner you have several bosses or customers, but you are also the boss of your employees.

Business owners own systems that allow the owner to be absent for long periods and still generate income.

Income diversification and taxes for business owners are similar to those of the self-employed. However, if the business is an corporation (S-Corp or C-Corp), not all income is subjected to the combined 15.3% FICA contribution, as is the case for the self-employed. For corporate entities, wages from working in the business are subject to FICA. The profit that is left after all expenses and salaries are paid is not subject to FICA.

*Since being a business owner is where a majority of the rich make their money, what are your plans to generate more income from this quadrant?*

## Investor – Cash Flow Quadrant

The last quadrant is Investor. As an investor it is all about having your money work for you. As an investor you can spread your investment money around to achieve greater income diversification, while lowing overall risk through less investment concentration.

There is an investment continuum related to taxes.

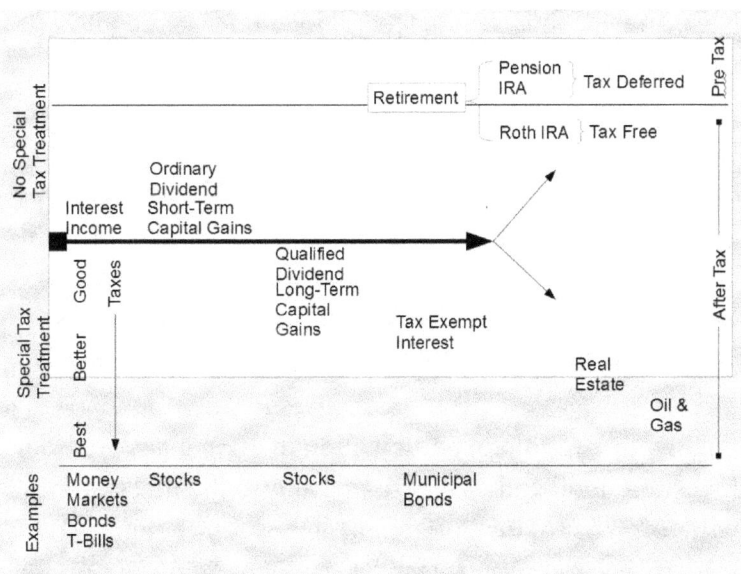

On one end of the investment continuum is interest income, where income comes from sources like money markets, bonds and T-bills. Ordinary dividends (like you receive as a business owner) and short term capital gains are also on this same end of the continuum. All these investments do not receive any special tax treatment.

However, moving along the continuum, there are qualified dividends and long-term capital gains that benefit from special tax treatment. Rather than being taxed based on how much you make, these investment vehicles are taxed for most investors at a fixed 15% rate. One exception is for the ultra rich, who pay 20%, which is far less that most investors' marginal income tax rate.

Next on the continuum is federal income tax-free interest income known as municipal bonds.

Beyond that there is income from real estate, which allows for depreciation to lower taxable income. Further capital gains, which are normally taxed when the property is sold, can be deferred indefinitely using what is known as a 1031 exchange. This allows the investor to grow their assets without paying capital gains on each successive transaction.

Finally, there is direct participation in oil and gas programs. Investing in oil and gas programs allows the investor to write off most of his investment against other sources of income, such as wages. Also, a depletion allowance makes only 85% of the income subject to taxes. However, to play in this game, most investors need to be accredited. This means that they have a net worth in excess of one million dollars or earn in excess of $250,000.00 per year.

*Since being an investor means your money works for you,*

*what are your plans to generate more income from this quadrant?*

# Business Evolution Series

Most business cultures follow a predictable path as the business progresses and grows. In addition to the business culture, the role of a business leader must also develop or the business gets stuck. Sometimes the founder adjusts his style or adds partners who have the skills the company needs.

Over the next four articles, we will look at the changing culture and leadership requirements a typical company passes through to see how a business develops. With respect to culture, the following table looks at the evolution of a business from start-up to maturity.

| Start-up | Maturity |
|---|---|
| Survival | Doing it Better |
| Few Meetings | Many Meetings |
| One Product/Service | Many Products/Services |
| Outwardly Focused | Inwardly Focused |
| Offensive | Defensive |
| Long Term Investments | Short Term Profits |
| Trend Setter | Trend Follower |
| Leadership | Management |
| Creative | Process |
| Risk Taker | Risk Adverse |
| Personal | Detached |

The role of the leader will evolve as the company progresses through four distinct phases. These phases will be covered over the next four articles.

*What cultural qualities does your business have?*

## *Stage 1: The Oracles of Business*

Stage 1 encompasses the pre-start up and early start-up period of a business.

A company is started by a founder who is essentially the idea person behind the business. I refer to this person as the "oracle." In classical antiquity, an oracle is a person who can see and predict the future. The oracle of a business is the charismatic and often eccentric person that plays a major role during stage 1 of the business development cycle.

He is often ineffective on his own since he is technically focused and lacks the essential business acumen to convert his ideas into a thriving business. The oracle is often not motivated by material comforts, but tends to be more motivated by the process of idea generation itself. They like to create a new product or service in response to a recognized problem in order to contribute to society. In contrast, a business founded with the sole purpose of making money rarely makes any significant contributions to the market place.

The most valued attribute of the oracle is their vision and ability to get others to see it too. Oracles frequently started out at larger corporations where their creativity was stifled. They often leave corporate life to start their own business because their previous boss would not listen to their ideas.

The oracles of McDonald's were Richard and Maurice McDonald. They had the vision that the car culture was coming and built a drive-in car hop restaurant to serve food quickly. They invented the flat top grill and replaced glasses, napkins, and silverware with paper cups, paper bags, and wrappers. They experimented with menu items and finally settled on nine of their most popular items. All their burgers were topped the same way to decrease the time between orders so they could deliver your meal as fast as possible.

Being idea guys, they got bored when they didn't see any more ways to improve. They did not have the passion or the skills for expansion. Businesses in stage 1 often have one product or service. Survival is the name of the game for these companies. Many businesses remain stuck at this point since it takes a different type of leader to move past stage 1.

Moving from one stage to the next is like changing gears in an automobile with an manual transmission; it requires a conscious effort and you may lose a little momentum during the change.

*Is your business stuck in stage 1?*

## Stage 2: The Generals of Business

For a business to advance from stage 1 to stage 2, the business requires that the role of the oracle be supported or replaced by a business development person. I refer to this new leader as the "general." In our McDonald's example from the previous article, it was a guy by the name of Ray Kroc who was the general. Ray Kroc bought the business from the McDonald brothers and took McDonald's from stage 1 to stage 2.

This cycle continues to repeat itself over and over for any business that continues to grow and evolve past basic survival mode.

Thomas Edison was an oracle. By himself, Edison invented many things. However, he was not capable of growing his inventions into a really profitable business. Edison didn't have the desire or skills to take his ideas beyond a stage 1 business and was always looking for funds to continue his research. It took the likes of JP Morgan, a general, to take Edison's ideas and turn them into the company we know today as GE.

Sometimes the oracle acquires the skills of the general, such as with the case of Henry Ford and JD Rockefeller. However, this is less common in more modern times.

Frequently, the oracle and general get paired up early in a company's life cycle based on the perceived strength and weaknesses of the founders. For example, Stephen Wozniak was the oracle and Steve Jobs was the general for Apple. Bill Hewlett was the oracle and David Packard was the general for the Hewlett-Pakard Company. Paul Allen was the oracle and Bill Gates was the general for Microsoft. You get the picture.

For many stage 1 businesses, the oracle sells either all or most of their business after they reach the limit of their skills. The business is then acquired by the general. For the general, expansion is the name of the game. For the general, their mission is clear and urgent. They like being in charge and making decisions.

The general is often accused of being authoritarian and not consulting others before making a decision. They have little patience for planning and administrative tasks. The business general, like their military counterpart, have undying loyalty from their followers based on their "take no prisoners" attitude. However, while generals are charismatic leaders, they are so focused on moving forward there is no time for any kind of succession planning. When business generals die or move on, their businesses often collapse without their leadership.

No one is there to pick up the flag after they are gone. Generals are motivated by a single goal and hard wired to excel during periods of crisis. However, when the objective is achieved, they fail to recognize or rise to subsequent challenges. At this point stage 2 has often gone as far as it can go and the the general needs to be replaced to move to stage 3.

*Are you a general of a stage 2 company?*

## Stage 3: The Athletes and Performers of Business

For a business to advance from stage 2 to stage 3, the business undergoes a substantial shift from being on the offensive and growth oriented to becoming more defensive and focused on process improvement through business segmentation.

The business segmentation associated with stage 3 sets up the business for shared leadership and management by creating multiple divisions.

In stage 3, true leadership begins to migrate more towards management. At stage 3, humanistic motives are being replaced by profit and wealth motives. Rank is introduced; there are workers, supervisor, managers, and vice presidents. The culture is changed from one of unity for a single purpose to becoming more about individualism.

On one side of the organization is the operations department, which is focused inwardly. I call the people who work in the operations department the "athletes." As in sports, business athletes are focused on doing one thing better than anyone else. Within the operations department, there are engineering athletes, manufacturing athletes, human resource athletes, and so on.

On the other side of the organization is the sales and

marketing department. I call the people who work in the sales and marketing department "performers." As with theater or screen performers, business performers are outwardly focused and focused on their audience.

Athletes share many traits of generals and often take over a division using general type skills by improving production and increasing specialization. However, athletes are more introverted than generals. Athletes enjoy the actual work, are obsessed with measuring progress, and do not like spending time talking in meetings. They like to make decisions and act quickly. However, they recognize they are not visionaries and focus on execution.

Performers are naturally more extroverted and often come from sales. Performers are convincing and enthusiastic communicators, feel more affinity towards the customer, and see their coworkers as obstacles to serving the customer. They love to keep score and are very competitive. Performers are often frustrated by the company's lack of expansion and feel there is way too much paperwork.

In stage 3, athletes and performers take over for the general. Henry Ford was a good example of a general that hung on too long and was surpassed by General Motors, a business that successfully transitioned to stage 3.

*Is your business a stage 3 business?*

## *Stage 4: The Guardians of Business*

When a business advances from stage 3 to stage 4, the business transformation is nearly complete. During stage 4, company decay really begins to set in and the administration of the business is placed in the hands of a "guardian."

The primary motives of the business guardian are comfort and security. Unity towards a purpose is absent and replaced with self interest. The layered class structures fail to understand each other; leaders and followers grow more distant. Workers doubt their leaders have any clear vision and are no longer willing to dedicate themselves to the company's mission. Workers are in it for the money and generally are just going through the motions. Internal harmony breaks down and the guardian increasingly seeks unfamiliar solutions to problems he does not fully understand.

The board of directors are indebted to the leadership and conform rather than challenge leadership. Guardians spend most of their time in meetings trying to understand what has or will go wrong. They believe tighter control will solve their problems, making matters even worse. They are more concerned with how Wall Street or the investors see the company than the customer.

Stage 4 companies become so inept in the industry they are challenged by start-ups and are frequent targets of acquisition by competitors.

Finally, the culture of a business in stage 4 is one of inaction and has achieved the same level of bureaucracy as our federal government.

The entire evolution of a business can be seen in the life cycle of Xerox. Chester Carlson invented copier technology and was the oracle. He spent nine years trying to sell the technology with no real progress. The company moved to stage 2 when Wilson Haloid, the general, took charge and funded research to turn the idea into the product we know as xerography. Enter Horace Becker, the athlete that managed engineering and manufacturing which turned xerography into a reliable product. Horace was succeeded by Joe Wilson, the performer that changed the model from selling to leasing, growing the company to be so large xerox became a virtual monopoly. Anti-trust suites were filed. Afraid to act, Xerox was taken over by lawyers and Xerox evolved into a bureaucratic culture under Peter McColough, the guardian.

*Do you work for a stage 4 business?*

*Is now the time to leave and become an entrepreneur?*

www.ingramcontent.com/pod-product-compliance
Lightning Source LLC
Chambersburg PA
CBHW070258190526
45169CB00001B/454